D0014340

Thoughts on

VIRTUE

Thoughts on VIRTUE

TRIUMPH BOOKS
CHICAGO

This edition is published by Triumph Books, Chicago,
by arrangement with Forbes Inc.

ISBN 1-57243-106-7 (cloth)

This book is available in quantity at special discounts for your group
or organization. For more information, contact:

TRIUMPH BOOKS
644 South Clark Street
Chicago, Illinois 60605
(312) 939-3330 FAX (312) 663-3557

Book design by Graffolio.
Cover design © 1996 by Triumph Books.
Illustration from the Dover Pictorial Archive Series,
edited by Jim Harter (Dover Publications), used with permission.

Printed in the United States of America.

Contents

INTRODUCTION

The moving motive in establishing FORBES Magazine, in 1917, was ardent desire to promulgate humaneness in business, then woefully lacking. . . .

Every issue of FORBES, since its inception, has appeared under the masthead: "With all thy getting, get understanding."

Not only so, but we have devoted, all through the years, a full page to "Thoughts on the Business of Life," reflections by ancient and modern sages calculated to inspire a philosophic mode of life, broad sympathies, charity towards all. . . .

I have faith that the time will eventually come when employees and employers, as well as all mankind, will realize that they serve themselves best when they serve others most.

B. C. Forbes

ADVERSITY

A single solitary philosopher
may be great, virtuous and happy
in the depth of poverty,
but not a whole people.

ISELIN

Adversity is the trial of principle.
Without it, a man hardly knows
whether he is honest or not.

HENRY FIELDING

The effect of great
and inevitable misfortune
is to elevate those souls
which it does not deprive of all virtue.

ELISABETH GUIZOT

Fresh air and innocence are good
if you don't take too much of them—
but I always remember
that most of the achievements
and pleasures of life
are in bad air.

OLIVER WENDELL HOLMES

Genuine morality is preserved
only in the school of adversity;
a state of continuous prosperity
may easily prove
a quicksand to virtue.

JOHANN SCHILLER

Adversity makes men;
good fortune makes monsters.

FRENCH PROVERB

I love the man
that can smile in trouble,
that can gather strength
from distress,
and grow brave by reflection.
'Tis the business
of little minds to shrink,
but he whose heart is firm,
and whose conscience
approves his conduct,
will pursue his principles
unto death.

THOMAS PAINE

In the adversity of our best friends
we often find something
that is not wholly displeasing to us.

FRANÇOIS LA ROCHEFOUCAULD

It is a hard rule of life,
and I believe a healthy one,
that no great plan is ever carried out
without meeting and overcoming
endless obstacles that come up
to try the skill of man's hand,
the quality of his courage,
and the endurance of his faith.

DONALD DOUGLAS

Who hath not known ill fortune,
never knew himself, or his own virtue.

MALLETT

The abundant life . . .
does not come to those
who have all obstacles removed
from their paths by others.
It develops from within
and is rooted in strong mental
and moral fiber.

WILLIAM MATHER LEWIS

The gem cannot be polished without friction,
nor man perfected without trials.

CHINESE PROVERB

The greatest object in the universe,
says a certain philosopher,
is a good man struggling with adversity;
yet there is still a greater,
which is the good man that comes to relieve it.

OLIVER GOLDSMITH

CHARACTER

A good name is seldom regained.
When character is gone,
all is gone,
and one of the richest jewels of life
is lost forever.

JOEL HAWES

A man need not extol his virtues,
nor comment on his failings,
his friends know the former,
and his enemies will search out the latter.

CHARLES B. ROGERS

Character is that
which reveals moral purpose,
exposing the class of things
a man chooses or avoids.

ARISTOTLE

Excellence is an art won
by training and habituation.
We do not act rightly
because we have virtue or excellence,
but we rather have those
because we have acted rightly.
We are what we repeatedly do.
Excellence, then, is not an act but a habit.

ARISTOTLE

Industry, economy, honesty and kindness
form a quartet of virtue
that will never be improved upon.

JAMES OLIVER

No longer talk at all
about the kind of man
a good man ought to be,
but be such.

MARCUS AURELIUS

No virtue
is more universally accepted
as a test of good character
than trustworthiness.

HARRY EMERSON FOSDICK

Of all virtues
magnanimity is the rarest;
there are a hundred persons of merit
for one who willingly acknowledges it
in another.

WILLIAM HAZLITT

The first great gift
we can bestow on others
is a good example.

THOMAS MORELL

The simple virtues
of willingness, readiness,
alertness and courtesy
will carry a man farther
than mere smartness.

DAVIDSON

The virtue of man
ought to be measured,
not by his extraordinary exertions,
but by his everyday conduct.

BLAISE PASCAL

To try too hard
to make people good
is one way to make them worse.
The only way
to make them good
is to be good,
remembering well
the beam and the mote.

GEORGE McDONALD

We can often do more
for other men
by correcting our own faults
than by trying to correct theirs.

FRANÇOIS FÉNELON

We learn our virtues
from the friends who love us;
our faults from the enemy
who hates us.
We cannot easily discover
our real character from a friend.
He is a mirror,
on which the warmth of our breath
impedes the clearness
of the reflection.

JEAN PAUL RICHTER

Without consistency
there is no moral strength.

ROBERT OWEN

Tell me with whom thou art found,
and I will tell thee who thou art.

JOHANN WOLFGANG VON GOETHE

As diamonds cut diamonds,
and one hone smooths a second,
all the parts of intellect
are whetstones to each other;
and genius,
which is but the result
of their mutual sharpening,
is character, too.

CYRUS A. BARTOL

CONSCIENCE

A quiet conscience
makes one so serene.

LORD BYRON

(GEORGE GORDON)

———

Conscience admonishes
as a friend
before punishing us
as a judge.

STANISLAUS LESZCYNSKI

———

Conscience is a coward,
and those faults
it has not strength to prevent,
it seldom has
justice enough to accuse.

OLIVER GOLDSMITH

Conscience is the root
of all true courage;
if a man would be brave
let him obey his conscience.

JAMES FREEMAN CLARKE

He who commits a wrong
will himself inevitably see
the writing on the wall,
though the world
may not count him guilty.

MARTIN TUPPER

He who sacrifices his conscience
to ambition
burns a picture
to obtain the ashes.

CHINESE PROVERB

If a dog will not come to you
after he has looked you in the face,
you ought to go home
and examine your conscience.

WOODROW WILSON

In matters of conscience,
first thoughts are best;
in matters of prudence,
last thoughts are best.

ROBERT HALL

It is not who is right,
but what is right,
that is of importance.

THOMAS H. HUXLEY

It is now evident
to all men of spiritual discernment
that healing of the world's woes
will not come through
this or that social or political theory;
not through violent changes
in government,
but in the still small voice
that speaks to the conscience
and the heart.

ARTHUR J. MOORE

Man's problem
in the last analysis
is man himself.
A man beset by evil within
and from without
can mobilize his spiritual resources
to conquer that evil.
Just so can the human race
mobilize its moral and spiritual power
to defeat the material power
of evil that threatens it.

RICHARD E. BYRD

Never let a man imagine
that he can pursue a good end
by evil means,
without sinning
against his own soul.
The evil effect on himself is certain.

ROBERT SOUTHEY

Reason often makes mistakes,
but conscience never does.

JOSH BILLINGS

The conscience of children
is formed by the influences
that surround them;
their notions of good and evil
are the result of the moral atmosphere
they breathe.

JEAN PAUL RICHTER

There is no witness so terrible—
no accuser so powerful
as conscience which dwells within us.

SOPHOCLES

Whatever is done without ostentation,
and without the people being witness of it,
is, in my opinion, most praiseworthy:
not that the public eye
should be entirely avoided,
for good actions
desire to be placed in the light;
but notwithstanding this,
the greatest theater for virtue
is conscience.

CICERO

COURAGE

A man of courage
is also full of faith.

CICERO

Courage, energy
and patience
are the virtues
which appeal to my heart.

FRITZ KREISLER

Courage is a quality
so necessary for maintaining virtue
that it is always respected,
even when it is associated with vice.

SAMUEL JOHNSON

Courage is a virtue
only so far as it is directed
to produce.

FRANÇOIS FÉNELON

Courage is the most common
and vulgar of the virtues.

HERMAN MELVILLE

Courage is the supreme virtue,
because it is the guarantor
of every other virtue.

BERGEN EVANS

Courage without conscience
is a wild beast.

RALPH INGERSOLL

Every man of courage
is a man of his word.

PIERRE CORNEILLE

Happy is he
who dares courageously
to defend what he loves.

OVID

It is curious that physical courage
should be so common in the world,
and moral courage so rare.

MARK TWAIN

The strongest, most generous
and proudest of all virtues
is courage.

MICHEL DE MONTAIGNE

Keep true,
never be ashamed of doing right;
decide on what you think is right,
and stick to it.

GEORGE ELIOT

Moral courage
is a virtue of higher cast
and nobler origin than physical.
It springs from a consciousness of virtue
and renders a man,
in the pursuit or defense of right,
superior to the fear of reproach,
opposition in contempt.

SAMUEL GOODRICH

Physical courage,
which despises all danger,
will make a man brave in one way;
and moral courage,
which despises all opinion,
will make a man brave in another.

CHARLES CALEB COLTON

The way of a superior man
is threefold:
virtuous, he is free from anxieties;
wise, he is free from perplexities;
bold, he is free from fear.

CONFUCIUS

True courage
is not the brutal force
of vulgar heroes,
but the firm resolve
of virtue and reason.

ALFRED NORTH WHITEHEAD

Whether you be man or woman
you will never do anything in this world
without courage.
It is the greatest quality of the mind
next to honor.

JAMES L. ALLEN

To see what is right,
and not do it,
is want of courage,
or of principle.

CONFUCIUS

Courage is what it takes
to stand up and speak;
courage is also what it takes
to sit down and listen.

WINSTON CHURCHILL

DISCIPLINE

A man without self-restraint
is like a barrel without hoops,
and tumbles to pieces.

HENRY WARD BEECHER

One may as well be asleep
as to read for anything
but to improve his mind and morals,
and regulate his conduct.

LAURENCE STERNE

Passions unguided
are for the most part
mere madness.

THOMAS HOBBES

Self-denial is not a virtue;
it is only the effect
of prudence on rascality.

GEORGE BERNARD SHAW

Talkers will refrain
from evil speaking
when listeners refrain
from evil hearing.

EDWARD GEORGE BULWER-LYTTON

To rule self
and subdue our passions
is the more praiseworthy
because so few know how to do it.

FRANCESCO GUICCIARDINI

Than self-restraint
there is nothing better.

LAO-TZU

That discipline
which corrects the eagerness
of worldly passions,
which fortifies the heart
with virtuous principles,
which enlightens the mind
with useful knowledge,
and furnishes to it
matter of enjoyment
from within itself,
is of more consequence
to real felicity
than all the provisions
which we can make
of the goods of fortune.

BLAIR

The highest proof of virtue
is to possess boundless power
without abusing it.

THOMAS B. MACAULAY

There is no memory with less satisfaction in it
than the memory of some temptation
we resisted.

JAMES BRANCH CABELL

Whoever yields to temptation
debases himself
with a debasement from which
he can never rise.
A man can be wronged and live;
but the unrestricted,
unchecked impulse to do wrong
is the first and second death.

HORACE MANN

When we live habitually
with the wicked,
we become necessarily
their victims or their disciples;
on the contrary,
when we associate with the virtuous
we form ourselves
in imitation of their virtues,
or at least lose, every day,
something of our faults.

AGAPET

EFFORT

A virtue and a muscle
are alike.
If neither of them is exercised
they get weak and flabby.

RICHARD L. ROONEY

Employment gives health,
sobriety, and morals.
Constant employment
and well-paid labor
produce . . . general prosperity,
content, and cheerfulness.

DANIEL WEBSTER

Every man is worth
just as much as the things
he busies himself with.

MARCUS AURELIUS

I see no virtues
where I smell no sweat.

FRANCIS QUARLES

If you pursue good with labor,
the labor passes away
but the good remains;
if you pursue evil with pleasure,
the pleasure passes away
and the evil remains.

CICERO

It is better to lay your life
upon the altar
of worthy endeavor
than to luxuriate and perish
as a weed.

ALBERT L. WILLIAMS

Life is a short day;
but it is a working day.
Activity may lead to evil,
but inactivity cannot lead to good.

HANNAH MORE

The door to virtue
is heavy and hard to push.

CHINESE PROVERB

The virtue of man
ought to be measured,
not by his extraordinary exertions,
but by his everyday conduct.

BLAISE PASCAL

Virtue
proceeds through effort.

EURIPIDES

Virtue,
though she gets her beginning
from nature,
yet receives her finishing touches
from learning.

QUINTILIAN

We are fallible.
We certainly haven't attained perfection.
But we can strive for it
and the virtue is in the striving.

CARLOS P. ROMULO

We often pray
for purity, unselfishness,
for the highest qualities of character,
and forget that these things
cannot be given,
but must be earned.

LYMAN ABBOTT

What is virtue?
Reason in practice.

J. J. DE CHENIER

When we are planning
for posterity,
we ought to remember
that virtue is not hereditary.

THOMAS PAINE

As long as the day lasts,
let's give it all we've got.

DAVID O. McKAY

He who finds diamonds
must grapple in mud and mire
because diamonds are not found
in polished stones.
They are made.

HENRY B. WILSON

Ideas must work
through the brains and the arms
of good and brave men,
or they are no better
than dreams.

RALPH WALDO EMERSON

No race can prosper
until it learns
that there is as much dignity
in tilling a field
as in writing a poem.

BOOKER T. WASHINGTON

ENTHUSIASM

A mother should give her children
a superabundance of enthusiasm,
that after they have lost
all they are sure to lose
on mixing with the world,
enough may still remain
to prompt and support them
through great actions.

JULIUS C. HARE

Enthusiasm is a virtue
rarely to be met with
in seasons of calm
and unruffled prosperity.

THOMAS CHALMERS

Enthusiasm
is the best protection
in any situation.
Wholeheartedness
is contagious.
Give yourself,
if you wish to get others.

DAVID SEABURY

Fires can't be made
with dead embers,
nor can enthusiasm be stirred
by spiritless men.
Enthusiasm in our daily work
lightens effort
and turns even labor
into pleasant tasks.

STANLEY BALDWIN

From the glow of enthusiasm
I let the melody escape.
I pursue it.
Breathless I catch up with it.
It flies again,
it disappears,
it plunges into a chaos
of diverse emotions.
I catch it again,
I seize it,
I embrace it with delight . . . .
I multiply it by modulations,
and at last I triumph
in the first theme.
There is the whole symphony.

LUDWIG VAN BEETHOVEN

I do not love a man
who is zealous for nothing.

OLIVER GOLDSMITH

I think there is some virtue
in eagerness,
whether its object
prove true or false.
How utterly dull
would be a wholly prudent man.

ALDO LEOPOLD

Zeal for the public good
is the characteristic
of a man of honor and a gentleman,
and must take the place
of pleasures, profits,
and all other private gratifications.

RICHARD STEELE

Let us recognize
the beauty and power
of true enthusiasm;
and whatever we may do
to enlighten ourselves or others,
guard against checking or chilling
a single earnest sentiment.

HENRY TUCKERMAN

———

Men are nothing
until they are excited.

MICHEL DE MONTAIGNE

———

No virtue is safe
that is not enthusiastic.

JOHN SEELEY

Nobody grows old
by merely living a number of years.
People grow old
only by deserting their ideals.
Years wrinkle the face,
but to give up enthusiasm
wrinkles the soul.

WATTERSON LOWE

Send the harmony of a Great Desire
vibrating through every fiber of your being.
Pray for a task
that will call forth your faith,
your courage, your perseverance,
and your spirit of sacrifice.
Keep your hands and your soul clean,
and the conquering current
will flow freely.

THOMAS DREIER

When enthusiasm
is inspired by reason,
controlled by caution,
sound in theory,
practical in application,
reflects confidence,
spreads good cheer,
raises morale,
inspires associates,
arouses loyalty,
and laughs at adversity,
it is beyond price.

COLEMAN COX

Men are nothing
until they are excited.

MICHEL DE MONTAIGNE

———

Youth must be optimistic.
Optimism is essential
to achievement
and it is also the foundation
of courage
and of true progress.

NICHOLAS MURRAY BUTLER

———

The world of achievement
has always belonged
to the optimist.

J. HAROLD WILKINS

Every man is valued
in this world
as he shows by his conduct
that he wishes
to be valued.

JEAN DE LA BRUYÈRE

GOODNESS

Between two evils,
choose neither;
between two goods,
choose both.

TYRON EDWARDS

⋯⋙⋘⋯

Good intentions
are very mortal
and perishable things;
like very mellow
and choice fruit
they are difficult to keep.

CHARLES SIMMONS

⋯⋙⋘⋯

Goodness is the only investment
which never fails.

HENRY DAVID THOREAU

Goodness consists
not in the outward things we do,
but in the inward thing we are.
To be good is the great thing.

EDWIN H. CHAPIN

He that is good
will infallibly become better,
and he that is bad
will as certainly become worse,
for vice, virtue and time
are three things
that never stand still.

CHARLES CALEB COLTON

He who stops being better
stops being good.

OLIVER CROMWELL

If we have need of a strong will
in order to do good,
it is still more necessary for us
in order not to do evil.

THOMAS MOLE

In the final analysis
there is no other solution
to man's progress
but the day's honest work,
the day's honest decisions,
the day's generous utterances
and the day's good deed.

CLARE BOOTH LUCE

It's so much easier to do good
than to be good.

B. C. FORBES

Nature does not bestow virtue;
to be good is an art.

SENECA

Τhe only reward of virtue
is virtue.

RALPH WALDO EMERSON

The world is good-natured
to people who are good-natured.

WILLIAM MAKEPEACE THACKERAY

There is virtue in country houses,
in gardens and orchards,
in fields, streams and groves,
in rustic recreations
and plain manners,
that neither cities
nor universities enjoy.

AMOS B. ALCOTT

Virtue is everywhere
that which is thought praiseworthy;
and nothing else but that
which has the allowance of public esteem
is called virtue.

JOHN LOCKE

Virtue
is its own reward.

CICERO

Whatever mitigates the woes
or increases the happiness of others—
this is my criterion of goodness.
And whatever injures society at large,
or any individual in it—
this is my measure of iniquity.

ROBERT BURNS

It is a great mistake
to think of being great
without goodness;
and I pronounce it as certain
that there was never yet
a truly great man
that was not at the same time
truly virtuous.

BENJAMIN FRANKLIN

It is far more important to me
to preserve an unblemished conscience
than to compass any object
however great.

WILLIAM ELLERY CHANNING

The only way
to compel men to speak good of us
is to do it.

VOLTAIRE

(FRANÇOIS MARIE AROUET)

HAPPINESS

An act of goodness is of itself
an act of happiness.
No reward coming after the event
can compare with the sweet reward
that went with it.

MAURICE MAETERLINCK

Doing good is the only certainly
happy action of a man's life.

SIR PHILIP SIDNEY

Good company
and good discourse
are the sinews of virtue.

IZAAK WALTON

Happiness
is a by-product of an effort
to make someone else happy.

GRETTA PALMER

If I had my life
to live over again,
I would have made a rule
to read some poetry
and listen to some music
at least once a week . . . .
The loss of these tastes
is a loss of happiness,
and may possibly be injurious
to the intellect,
and more probably
to the moral character.

CHARLES DARWIN

He who is virtuous
is wise;
and he who is wise
is good;
and he who is good
is happy.

BOETHIUS

If virtue promises happiness,
prosperity and peace,
then progress in virtue
is progress in each of these;
for to whatever point
the perfection of anything brings us,
progress is always
an approach toward it.

EPICTETUS

In dealings between man and man,
truth, sincerity and integrity
are of the utmost importance
to the felicity of life.

BENJAMIN FRANKLIN

One should seek virtue
for its own sake
and not from hope or fear,
or any external motive.
It is in virtue
that happiness consists,
for virtue is the state of mind
which tends to make
the whole of life harmonious.

ZENO

Our greatest happiness
does not depend
on the condition of life
in which chance has placed us,
but is always the result
of a good conscience, good health,
occupation, and freedom
in all just pursuits.

THOMAS JEFFERSON

There is no happiness
in wickedness.

EZRA TAFT BENSON

The happiness of your life
depends upon the quality
of your thoughts:
therefore, guard accordingly,
and take care that you entertain
no notions unsuitable to virtue
and reasonable nature.

MARCUS AURELIUS

There are two worlds:
the world that we can measure
with line and rule,
and the world that we feel
with our hearts and imaginations.

LEIGH HUNT

What is called virtue
in the common sense of the word
has nothing to do
with this or that man's prosperity,
or even happiness.

JAMES A. FROUDE

Every heart
that has beat strong and cheerfully
has left a hopeful impulse
behind it in the world,
and bettered the tradition
of mankind.

ROBERT LOUIS STEVENSON

HONESTY

Honest men fear
neither the light
nor the dark.

THOMAS FULLER

Honesty isn't any policy at all;
it's a state of mind
or it isn't honesty.

EUGENE L'HOTE

I hope I shall always possess
firmness and virtue
enough to maintain
what I consider the most enviable
of all titles,
the character of
the "Honest Man."

GEORGE WASHINGTON

If self-knowledge
is the road to virtue,
so is virtue
still more the road
to self-knowledge.

JEAN PAUL RICHTER

If we expect and demand
virtue and honor in others,
the flame of both
must burn brightly within ourselves
and shed their light
to illuminate the erstwhile dark corners
of distrust and dishonesty.

JAMES F. BELL

Lying
is a hateful and accursed vice.
We have no other tie
upon one another,
but our word.
If we did but discover
the horror and consequences of it,
we should pursue it
with fire and sword,
and more justly
than other crimes.

MICHEL DE MONTAIGNE

Make yourself an honest man,
and then you may be sure
that there is one less rascal
in the world.

THOMAS CARLYLE

Most men admire virtue,
who follow not her lore.

JOHN MILTON

Sincerity and truth
are the basis of every virtue.

CONFUCIUS

Suspicion
is far more apt to be wrong
than right;
oftener unjust
than just.
It is no friend to virtue,
and always an enemy
to happiness.

HOSEA BALLOU

Suspicion
is no less an enemy to virtue
than to happiness.
He that is already corrupt
is naturally suspicious,
and he that becomes suspicious
will quickly be corrupt.

SAMUEL JOHNSON

The first virtue
of all really great men
is that they are sincere.
They eradicate hypocrisy
from their hearts.
They bravely unveil their weaknesses,
their doubts, their defects.
They are courageous.

ANATOLE FRANCE

Honor

Any one entrusted with power
will abuse it if not also animated
with the love of truth and virtue,
no matter whether he be a prince,
or one of the people.

JEAN DE LA FONTAINE

Great souls
are always loyally submissive,
reverent to what is over them:
only small mean souls
are otherwise.

THOMAS CARLYLE

It seldom pays
to be rude.
It never pays
to be half rude.

NORMAN DOUGLAS

It is heaven upon earth
to have a man's mind
move in charity,
rest in providence
and turn upon the poles
of truth.

FRANCIS BACON

Liberal education
develops a sense of right,
duty and honor;
and more and more
in the modern world,
large business rests on rectitude
and honor as well
as on good judgment.

CHARLES W. ELIOT

Men show no mercy
and expect no mercy,
when honor calls,
or when they fight
for their idols or their gods.

JOHANN SCHILLER

The more virtuous
any man is,
the less easily
does he suspect others
to be vicious.

CICERO

Our inheritance of well-founded,
slowly conceived codes of honor,
morals and manners,
the passionate convictions
which so many hundreds of millions
share together
of the principles of freedom and justice,
are far more precious to us
than anything which scientific discoveries
could bestow.

WINSTON CHURCHILL

To be ambitious of true honor,
of the true glory and perfection
of our natures,
is the very principle
and incentive of virtue.

SIR PHILIP SIDNEY

Set the course of your lives
by the three stars—
sincerity, courage, unselfishness.
From these flow a host
of other virtues . . .
He who follows them
and does not seek success,
will attain the highest type of success,
that which lies in the esteem
of those among whom he dwells.

MONROE E. DEUTSCH

Those who educate children well
are more to be honored
than parents,
for these only gave life,
those the art of living well.

ARISTOTLE

The sages
do not consider
that making no mistakes
is a blessing.
They believe, rather,
that the great virtue of man
lies in his ability
to correct his mistakes
and continually make
a new man of himself.

WANG YANG-MING

Credit is like
a looking glass, which,
when once sullied by a breath,
may be wiped clear again,
but if once cracked
can never be repaired.

SIR WALTER SCOTT

Virtue and decency
are so nearly related
that it is difficult to separate them
from each other
but in our imagination.

CICERO

The shortest and surest way
to live with honor in the world
is to be in reality
what we would appear to be;
and if we observe, we shall find
that all human virtues
increase and strengthen themselves
by the practice and experience of them.

SOCRATES

To honor with hymns
and panegyrics
those who are still alive
is not safe;
a man should run his course
and make a fair ending,
and then we will praise him;
and let praise be given equally
to women as well as men
who have been distinguished
in virtue.

PLATO

You will find it less easy
to uproot faults
than to choke them
by gaining virtues.
Do not think of your faults,
still less of other's faults.
In every person who comes near you
look for what is good and strong;
honor that;
try to imitate it,
and your faults will drop off
like dead leaves
when their time comes.

JOHN RUSKIN

HUMILITY

By humility
I mean not the abjectness of a base mind,
but a prudent care
not to overvalue ourselves.

NATHANIEL CREW

Do not imagine yourself
to have what you have not;
but take full account
of the excellencies which you possess,
and in gratitude remember
how you would hanker after them,
if you had them not.

MARCUS AURELIUS

Great thoughts,
like great deeds,
need no trumpet.

JAMES M. BAILEY

Humility is a virtue all preach,
none practice,
and yet everybody is content to hear.

JOHN SELDON

Humility is the most difficult
of all virtues to achieve;
nothing dies harder
than the desire
to think well of self.

T. S. ELIOT

Humility leads to strength
and not to weakness.
It is the highest form of self-respect
to admit mistakes
and to make amends for them.

JOHN J. McCLOY

No man or woman
of the humblest sort
can really be strong,
gentle and good,
without the world being better for it,
without somebody being helped
and comforted by the very existence
of that goodness.

PHILLIPS BROOKS

One must become
as humble as the dust
before he can discover truth.

MAHATMA GANDHI

Only have enough
of little virtues and common fidelities,
and you need not mourn
because you are neither a hero
or a saint.

HENRY WARD BEECHER

Pride is a form
of selfishness.

DAVID LAWRENCE

Pride is a fruitful source
of uneasiness.
It keeps the mind in disquiet.
Humility is the antidote
to this evil.

LYDIA SIGOURNEY

The fruits of humility
are love and peace.

HEBREW PROVERB

The virtues
which keep this world sweet
and the faithfulness
which keeps it steadfast
are chiefly those
of the average man.
The danger of the two-talent man
is that he will be content
with mediocrity.

W. RUSSELL BOWIE

The work
an unknown good man has done
is like a vein of water
flowing hidden underground,
secretly making the ground green.

THOMAS CARLYLE

There is something in humility
which strangely exalts the heart.

ST. AUGUSTINE

We are apt to love praise,
but not to deserve it.
But if we would deserve it,
we must love virtue
more than that.

WILLIAM PENN

It is easy to look down on others;
to look down on ourselves
is the difficulty.

LORD PETERBOROUGH

(CHARLES MORDAUNT)

Life is a long lesson
in humility.

JAMES M. BARRIE

Sense shines
with a double luster
when it is set in humility.
An able and yet humble man
is a jewel worth a kingdom.

WILLIAM PENN

JUSTICE

Be fair.
Treat the other man
as you would be treated.

EVERETT W. LORD

⚬⚬⚬

By the just
we mean that which is lawful
and that which is fair
and equitable.

ARISTOTLE

⚬⚬⚬

Justice
is a certain rectitude of mind
whereby a man does
what he ought to do
in circumstances
confronting him.

SAINT THOMAS AQUINAS

I hate all bungling
as I do sin,
but particularly bungling in politics,
which leads to the misery and ruin
of many thousands and millions
of people.

JOHANN WOLFGANG VON GOETHE

Let us keep our mouths shut
and our pens dry
until we know the facts.

A. J. CARLSON

Nothing can be truly great
which is not right.

SAMUEL JOHNSON

Righteousness,
or *justice*, is,
undoubtedly of all the virtues,
the surest foundation
on which to create
and establish a new state.
But there are two nobler virtues,
industry and *frugality*,
which tend more to increase
the wealth, power and grandeur
of the community,
than all the others without them.

BENJAMIN FRANKLIN

The aim of justice
is to give everyone his due.

CICERO

———✦———

Since nothing is settled
until it is settled right,
no matter how unlimited power
a man may have,
unless he exercises it fairly and justly
his actions will return
to plague him.

FRANK A. VANDERLIP

———✦———

Those who deny
freedom to others
deserve it not for themselves
and, under a just God,
cannot long retain it.

ABRAHAM LINCOLN

We need justice.
We need toleration, honesty
and moral courage.
These are modern virtues
without which we cannot hope
to control the forces
science has let loose among us.

I. A. R. WYLIE

We ought always
to deal justly,
not only with those
who are just to us,
but likewise to those
who endeavor to injure us;
and this,
for fear lest by rendering them
evil for evil,
we should fall into the same vice.

HIEROCLES

KINDNESS

All values in this world
are more or less questionable,
but the most important thing in life
is human kindness.

YEVGENY YEVTUSHENKO

An effort made
for the happiness of others
lifts us above ourselves.

LYDIA M. CHILD

Goodwill for a business
is built by good goods,
service and truthful advertising.

MORRISON WAITE

Goodwill
is the mightiest practical force
in the universe.

CHARLES F. DOLE

Guard within yourself
that treasure kindness.
Know how to give
without hesitation,
how to lose
without regret,
how to acquire
without meanness.

GEORGE SAND

I wonder why it is
that we are not all kinder to each other
than we are.
How much the world needs it!
How easily it is done!

HENRY DRUMMOND

If a man be gracious to strangers,
it shows that he is a citizen of the world,
and his heart is no island,
cut off from other islands,
but a continent that joins them.

FRANCIS BACON

The best portion of a good man's life
is his little, nameless, unremembered
acts of kindness and of love.

WILLIAM WORDSWORTH

In modern life
nothing produces such an effect
as a good platitude.
It makes the whole world kind.

OSCAR WILDE

Of all the virtues
necessary to the completion
of the perfect man,
there is none to be more delicately implied
and less ostentatiously vaunted
than that of exquisite feeling
or universal benevolence.

EDWARD GEORGE BULWER-LYTTON

Small kindnesses,
small courtesies,
small considerations,
habitually practiced
in our social intercourse,
give a greater charm to the character
than the display of great talent
and accomplishments.

KELTY

When you find yourself overpowered,
as it were, by melancholy,
the best way is to go out
and do something kind
to somebody or other.

KEBLE

LOVE

Hating people
is like burning down your own house
to get rid of a rat.

HARRY EMERSON FOSDICK

Hatreds
are the cinders of affection.

SIR WALTER RALEIGH

He that falls in love with himself
will have no rivals.

BENJAMIN FRANKLIN

He who cannot love
must learn to flatter.

JOHANN WOLFGANG VON GOETHE

I believe that love
is the greatest thing in the world;
that it alone
can overcome hate;
that right can and will
triumph over might.

JOHN D. ROCKEFELLER, JR.

It is not love of self
but hatred of self
which is at the root of the troubles
that afflict our world.

ERIC HOFFER

Just remember
the world is not a playground
but a schoolroom.
Life is not a holiday
but an education.
One eternal lesson for us all:
to teach us how better
we should love.

BARBARA JORDAN

———

Love means
to love that which is unlovable,
or it is no virtue at all.

G. K. CHESTERTON

———

Love is clutched at
in preference to the laborious process
of changing from within.

KAREN HORNEY

Most men know what they hate,
few what they love.

CHARLES CALEB COLTON

———◆———

Of all earthly music,
that which reaches farthest into heaven
is the beating of a truly loving heart.

HENRY WARD BEECHER

———◆———

There is no remedy for love
but to love more.

HENRY DAVID THOREAU

———◆———

There is no way
under the sun
of making a man worthy of love,
except by loving him.

THOMAS MERTON

You cannot express hatred
for anything or anybody
unless you make use
of the supply of hatred within yourself.
The only hatred you can express
is your own personal possession.
To hate is to be enslaved by evil.

THOMAS DREIER

PRINCIPLES

As civilization progresses,
we should improve our laws basically,
not superficially.
Many things that are lawful
are highly immoral
and some things which are moral
are unlawful.

HENRY L. DOHERTY

Because his wife
is of such a delicate nature,
a man avoids using certain words
all through his married life,
and then one day he picks up
a bestseller she is reading
and finds five of the words
in the first chapter.

WILLIAM FEATHER

Blessed is he
who carries within himself
a God,
an ideal,
and who obeys it.

LOUIS PASTEUR

Each of us
is an impregnable fortress
that can be laid waste
only from within.

TIMOTHY J. FLYNN

Great ideals and principles
do not live from generation to generation
just because they are right,
nor even because
they have been carefully legislated.
Ideals and principles
continue from generation to generation
only when they are built
into the hearts of the children
as they grow up.

GEORGE S. BENSON

He who merely knows right principles
is not equal to him
who loves them.

CONFUCIUS

It requires greater virtues
to support good
than bad fortune.

FRANÇOIS LA ROCHEFOUCAULD

Nothing is politically right
which is morally wrong.

DANIEL O'CONNELL

Nothing sublimely artistic
has ever arisen out of mere art,
any more than anything
essentially reasonable
has ever arisen out of the pure reason.
There must always be
a rich moral soil
for any great aesthetic growth.

G. K. CHESTERTON

Principle—
particularly moral principle—
can never be a weathervane,
spinning around this way and that
with the shifting winds of expediency.
Moral principle is a compass
forever fixed and forever true.

EDWARD R. LYMAN

The best and noblest lives
are those which are set
toward high ideals.

RENÉ ALEMERAS

The foundations of the world
will be shaky
until the moral props
are restored.

ANNE O'HARE McCORMICK

The principles we live by,
in business and in social life,
are the most important part of happiness.
We need to be careful,
upon achieving happiness,
not to lose the virtues
which have produced it.

HARRY HARRISON

The soul that companies with virtue
is like an ever-flowing source.
It is a pure, clear,
and wholesome draught,
sweet, rich and generous of its store,
that injures not, neither destroys.

EPICTETUS

There can be no high civility
without a deep morality.

RALPH WALDO EMERSON

———◆———

Though conditions have grown puzzling
in their complexity,
though changes have been vast,
yet we may remain absolutely sure
of one thing;
that now as ever in the past,
and as it will ever be in the future,
there can be no substitute
for elemental virtues,
for the elemental qualities
to which we allude
when we speak of a man,
not only as a good man,
but as emphatically a man.

THEODORE ROOSEVELT

To live in the presence
of great truths and eternal laws,
to be led by permanent ideals—
that is what keeps a man patient
when the world ignores him,
and calm and unspoiled
when the world praises him.

HONORÉ DE BALZAC

What lies behind us
and what lies before us
are tiny matters
compared to what lies within us.

WILLIAM MORROW

Expedients are for the hour,
but principles are for the ages.
Just because the rains descend,
and the winds blow,
we cannot afford to build
on shifting sands.

HENRY WARD BEECHER

Many men do not allow
their principles to take root,
but pull them up
every now and then,
as children do to flowers
they have planted,
to see if they are growing.

HENRY WADSWORTH LONGFELLOW

RESPONSIBILITY

Every person is responsible
for all the good
within the scope of his abilities,
and for no more,
and none can tell
whose sphere is the largest.

GAIL HAMILTON

Hold yourself responsible
for a higher standard
than anybody else expects of you.
Never excuse yourself.
Never pity yourself.
Be a hard master to yourself—
and be lenient to everybody else.

HENRY WARD BEECHER

If you do what you should not,
you must bear what you would not.

BENJAMIN FRANKLIN

———

It is an old saying,
and one of fearful and fathomless import,
that we are forming characters for eternity.
Forming characters? Whose?
Our own or others?
Both—and in that momentous act
lies the peril and responsibility
of our existence.

ELIHU BURRITT

Man is still responsible . . .
His success lies
not with the stars
but with himself.
He must carry on the fight
of self-correction and discipline.
He must fight mediocrity as sin
and live against the imperative
of life's highest ideal.

FRANK CURTIS WILLIAMS

Provision for others
is a fundamental responsibility
of human life.

WOODROW WILSON

Responsibility for the creation
of the good world
in which the good life may be realized,
which the frustrated ages of the past
loaded upon the gods,
is now being assumed by man.

A. EUSTACE HAYDON

The great task of the peace
is to work morals into it.
The only sort of peace that will be real
is one in which everybody takes his share
of responsibility.

SIR FREDRICK EGGLESTON

To many people
virtue consists chiefly in repenting faults,
not in avoiding them.

GEORG C. LICHTENBERG

There is little pleasure in the world
that is true and sincere
beside the pleasure
of doing our duty and doing good.

JOHN TILLOTSON

To preserve health
is a moral and religious duty,
for health is the basis of all social virtues.
We can no longer be useful
when not well.

SAMUEL JOHNSON

What do I owe to my times,
to my country, to my neighbors,
to my friends?
Such are the questions which a virtuous man
ought often to ask himself.

JOHANN LAVATER

SERVICE

Do all the good you can,
in all the ways you can,
to all the souls you can,
in every place you can,
at all the times you can,
with all the zeal you can,
as long as ever you can.

JOHN WESLEY

The soldier who dies
to save his brothers
reaches the highest
of all degrees of charity,
and this is the virtue
of a single act of charity:
It cancels a whole lifetime
of sin.

CARDINAL MERCIER

Get all you can
without hurting your soul,
your body, or your neighbor.
Save all you can,
cutting off every needless expense.
Give all you can.
Be glad to give,
and ready to distribute;
laying up in store for yourselves
a good foundation
against the time to come,
that you may attain eternal life.

JOHN WESLEY

No one has learned
the meaning of life
until he has surrendered his ego
to the service of his fellow men.

BERAN WOLFE

Philanthropy [has become]
simply the refuge of people
who wish to annoy their fellow creatures.

OSCAR WILDE

Service is the rent
that we pay for our room on earth.

LORD HALIFAX

Service to a just cause
rewards the worker
with more real happiness and satisfaction
than any other venture of life.

CARRIE CHAPMAN CATT

The true measure of a man
is not the number of servants he has,
but the number of people he serves.

ARNOLD GLASGOW

The vocation of every man and woman
is to serve other people.

LEO TOLSTOI

There is but one virtue—
the eternal sacrifice of self.

GEORGE SAND

To devote a portion of one's leisure
to doing something for someone else
is one of the highest forms of recreation.

GERALD B. FITZGERALD

To give real service
you must add something
which cannot be bought or measured with money,
and that is sincerity and integrity.

DONALD A. ADAMS

Try to forget yourself
in the service of others.
For when we think too much of ourselves
and our own interests,
we easily become despondent.
But when we work for others,
our efforts return to bless us.

SIDNEY POWELL

When a person is down in the world,
an ounce of help is better
than a pound of preaching.

EDWARD GEORGE BULWER-LYTTON

TOLERANCE

Anger, if not restrained,
is frequently more hurtful to us
than the injury that provokes it.

SENECA

Anger is the most impotent of passions.
It effects nothing it goes about,
and hurts the one who is possessed by it
more than the one
against whom it is directed.

LORD CLARENDON

(EDWARD HYDE)

Give a good deed
the credit of a good motive;
and give an evil deed
the benefit of the doubt.

BRANDER MATTHEWS

Half the secret
of getting along with people
is consideration of their views;
the other half is tolerance
in one's own views.

DANIEL FROHMAN

He is happy
whose circumstances
suit his temper;
but he is more excellent
who can suit his temper
to any circumstances.

DAVID HUME

He that cannot forgive others,
breaks the bridge
over which he must pass himself;
for every man
has need to be forgiven.

LORD HERBERT

The worst counterfeit of tolerance
is the sheer self-interest which argues
that we want others to have a good time
when in reality our real motive
is that others may think well of us.

RALPH W. SOCKMAN

I believe with all my heart
that civilization has produced
nothing finer than a man or woman
who thinks and practices
true tolerance.
Some one has said
that most of us don't think,
we just occasionally
rearrange our prejudices.
And I suspect that even today . . .
the quality of true tolerance
is as rare as the quality of mercy.

FRANK KNOX

It is not a merit to tolerate,
but rather a crime
to be intolerant.

PERCY BYSSHE SHELLEY

I've never any pity
for conceited people,
because I think they carry their comfort
about with them.

GEORGE ELIOT

Tolerance comes with age.
I see no fault committed
that I myself could not have committed
at some time or other.

JOHANN WOLFGANG VON GOETHE

Tolerance consists
of seeing certain things with your heart
instead of with you eyes.

ORLANDO A. BATTISTA

Tolerance
is the positive and cordial effort
to understand another's beliefs,
practices, and habits
without necessarily sharing
or accepting them.

JOSHUA L. LIEBMAN

A leaf that is destined to grow large
is full of grooves and wrinkles
at the start.
Now if one has no patience
and wants it smooth offhand
like a willow leaf,
there is trouble ahead

JOHANN WOLFGANG VON GOETHE

Toleration is good for all
or it is good for none.

EDMUND BURKE

To feel much for others
and little for ourselves;
to restrain our selfishness
and exercise our benevolent affections,
constitute the perfection
of human nature.

ADAM SMITH

Vice

Better shun the bait
than struggle in the snare.

JOHN DRYDEN

———

Delusions, errors and lies
are like huge, gaudy vessels,
the rafters of which
are rotten and worm-eaten,
and those who embark in them
are fated to be shipwrecked.

BUDDHA

———

Like gluttony or drunkenness,
hatred seems an agreeable vice
when you practice it yourself,
but disgusting when observed in others.

WILLIAM H. IRWIN

He that has energy enough
to root out a vice,
should go further,
and try to plant a virtue
in its place;
otherwise he will have his labor
to renew.
A strong soil
that has produced weeds
may be made
to produce wheat.

CHARLES CALEB COLTON

It has ever been my experience
that folks who have no vices
have very few virtues.

ABRAHAM LINCOLN

If you ask me
which is the real hereditary sin
of human nature,
do you imagine
I shall answer pride, or luxury,
or ambition, or egotism?
No; I shall say indolence.
Who conquers indolence
will conquer all the rest.
Indeed all good principles
must stagnate without mental activity.

JOHANN ZIMMERMAN

Misfortune
does not always wait on vice;
nor is success the constant guest
of virtue.

WILLIAM HAVARD

Prejudice is not held against people
because they have evil qualities.
Evil qualities are imputed to people
because prejudices are held against them.

MARSHALL WINGFIELD

Purity of soul
cannot be lost
without consent.

ST. AUGUSTINE

Sometimes we may learn more
from a man's errors
than from his virtues.

HENRY WADSWORTH LONGFELLOW

There can be no such thing
as a necessary evil.
For, if a thing is really necessary,
it cannot be an evil
and if it is an evil,
it is not necessary.

TIORIO

Those who cause divisions,
in order to injure other people,
are in fact preparing pitfalls
for their own ruin.

CHINESE PROVERB

To persist in doing wrong
extenuates not the wrong,
but makes it much more heavy.

WILLIAM SHAKESPEARE

Virtue by calculation
is the virtue of vice.

JOSEPH JOUBERT

What is evil?—
Whatever springs from weakness.

FRIEDRICH W. NIETZSCHE

No man
has become very wicked
all at once.

JUVENAL

It is always with the best intentions
that the worst work is done.

OSCAR WILDE

There is no happiness
in wickedness.

EZRA TAFT BENSON

The wicked are wicked, no doubt,
and they go astray
and they fall,
and they come back
by their desserts,
but who can tell the mischief
which the very virtuous do?

WILLIAM MAKEPEACE THACKERAY

INDEX